Copyright © 2022 Emily Olstein

No part of this publication may be reproduced in whole, or in part, or stored in a retrieval system, or transmitted in any form, or by any means, electronic, mechanical, photocopying, recording, or otherwise, without written permission of the author.
Composition by Toby Mikle of MyBookIllustrator.com

WHEN I WAS BORN

Written by Emily Olstein

Artwork by Toby Mikle

I am truly special, because I have two mommies.

I lived in first mom's tummy till I grew big and strong.

Then birth-time is when Forever Mom came along.

NURSERY ROOM

Wrapped safe and warm, a nurse
handed me to Forever Mom.

Her face glowed with happiness –
love flowed from her heart.

I was cherished. I was wanted.
Her special sweetheart.

"You're brave!" Forever Mom said. "I will treasure this gift."

My birth mom sighed softly, "It is the best thing to do."

Forever Mom whispered, "Dreams do really come true."

I needed a nap, because
being born is hard work.

"See you later, sweet child,"
my forever mom said.

Then bottled and diapered,
I fell asleep in my bed.

Two days later, I was on my way to my grandparents.

"We must stay here little one, till your adoption's complete."

Smiling down at me, Forever Mom tickled my feet.

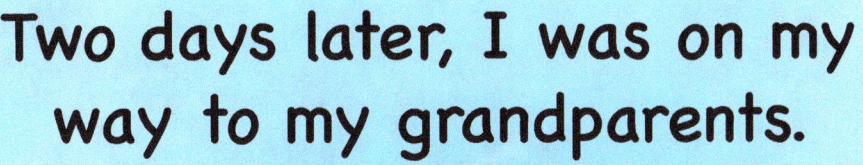

After that, Grandpa held me; his arms wrapped me with love.

"We are so blessed to have you," he said well-wishing.

"We'll go to the park and I'll take you fishing."

Forever Mom took me back. She kissed my cheek and laughed.

"It'll be a while, Grandpa, before our boy walks and plays."

"Just be here, and for now show him how to stargaze."

"I was adopted too," Forever Mom whispered one night.

"My parents longed for a child, just as I longed for YOU!"

"And thanks to dreams and prayers, it's finally come true!"

I also had a big brother – he and Dad phoned each day.

He wanted to know when I'd be big enough to play?

"Be patient," said Forever Mom. "That's a long time away."

With the adoption complete,
we drove to our home town,

Where Dad and my brother
waited to welcome me there.

Giving kisses and cuddles – it
was a love-fest affair!

I know now that babies must
have love and good care.

There are many fine moms and
dads who long for a child.

And my parents are awesome. . .
whether I'm sweet or wild!

They "chose" me for our family,
and I'm so glad they did.

You're "extra special" for sure,
if you're an ADOPTED KID!

CPSIA information can be obtained
at www.ICGtesting.com
Printed in the USA
JSHW031351051222
33633JS00002B/140